Under the Sea Song Book

Frances Turnbull

Copyright © 2018 Frances Turnbull

Under the Sea Song Book
All rights reserved
Musicaliti Publishing, Bolton, UK

ISBN: 978-1907935800

www.musicaliti.co.uk

Contents

Ukulele Tuning and Chords	4
Sad Crab	6
Squire Squid	10
Shy Shark	14
Green Fish	18
Little Red Fish	22
Starfish	26
Turtle	30
Octopus	34
Seahorse	38
Whale	42
All characters	46
Write your own song	47

Ukulele Chords

Ukuleles are small, accessible and relatively cheap instruments that can be used to play the accompaniment to many songs.

Each string should be tuned to specific notes (can be found on tuned instruments like xylophones, pianos or recorders etc.). The standard ukulele tuning is:

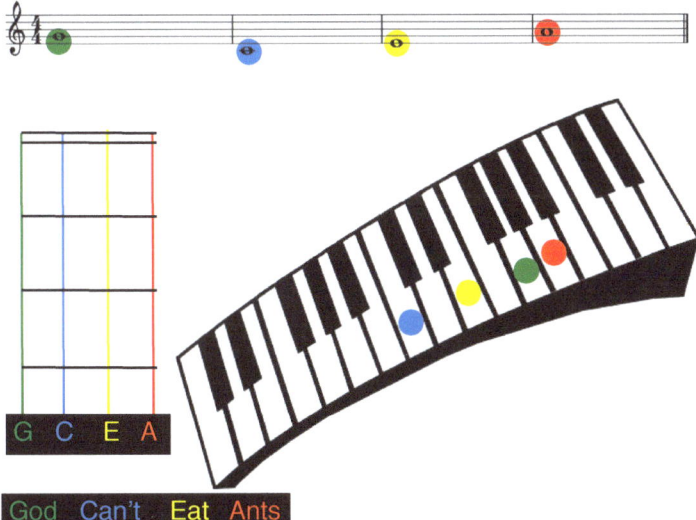

By placing your fingers on the frets at the positions on the pictures, (between the lines), you change the sound of the strings into chords when strummed altogether.

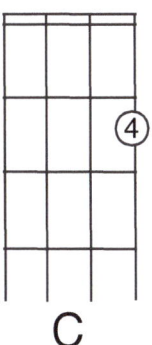
C

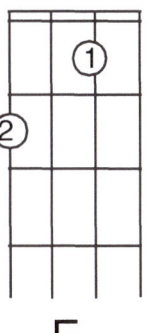
F

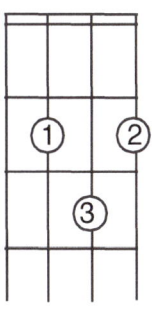
G

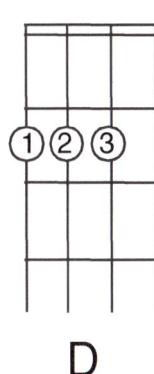
D

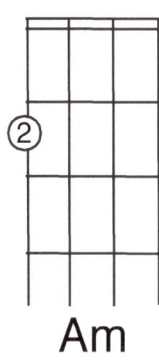
Am

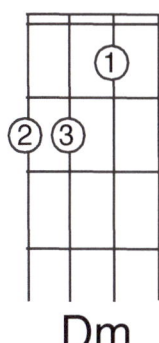
Dm

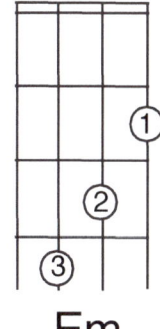
Em

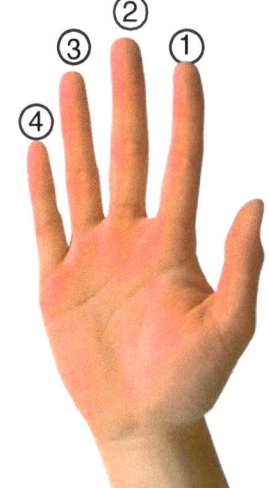

Under the Sea Song Book

Once upon a time, in the ocean blue, deep, deep down below ...

Frances Turnbull

sad crab
zig zag
sad crab
zig zag
sad crab
zig zag

Under the Sea Song Book

Once upon a time, there was a lovely creature called Sad Crab, who lived in the ocean blue.

Her biggest dream was to seek her fortune by going on a Great Adventure with a posse of friends!

But she had no friends because she was shy. Feeling very sad one day, she made up a little dance.

Zig-zag-zig-zag went her little clawed feet - zig-zag-zig-zag to the ocean beat!

Frances Turnbull

Sad Crab Zig Zag
Under the Sea

Composer: F. Turnbull

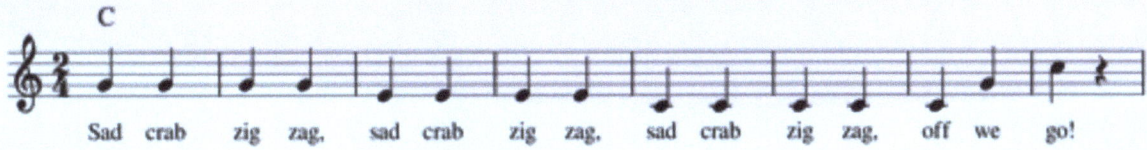

Sad crab zig zag, sad crab zig zag, sad crab zig zag, off we go!

Sad crab zig zag, sad crab zig zag, sad crab zig zag, off we go!

Sad crab zig zag, sad crab zig zag, sad crab zig zag, off we go!

Sad crab zig zag, sad crab zig zag, sad crab zig zag, off we go!

Under the Sea Song Book

Meet the ...
Squire Squid

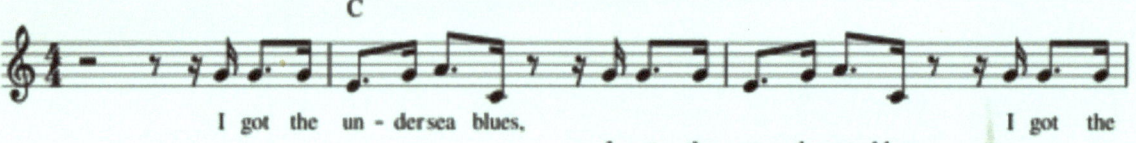

Under Sea Blues
Under the Sea

Arranged by: F. Turnbull

I got the un-dersea blues, I got the un-dersea blues, I got the

un-dersea blues I got the un-dersea blues, I got the un-dersea blues I got the

un-dersea blues, I got the un-dersea blues I got the un-dersea blues I'm gon-na / I'm gon-na

tap, tap, tap my blues a-way, I got the un-dersea blues!
tap, tap, tap my blues a-way, I got the un-dersea blues!

la la la la

la la la la

One fine day, as Sad Crab zig-zagged across the ocean floor, she noticed a very timid creature peaking out from behind the seaweed.

Squire Squid was very nervous around new friends, but when no-one was around, he danced and played in the water like an elegant dancer, swirling and twirling gracefully, swirling and twirling for all to see.

Sad Crab had crawled under a rock, and watched the whole show. She told Squire Squid that she needed the best dancer on her Great Adventure, and that Squire Squid was the best she had seen.

Straight away, Squire Squid agreed to join the Great Adventure!

Frances Turnbull

Squire Squid
Under the Sea

Composer: F. Turnbull

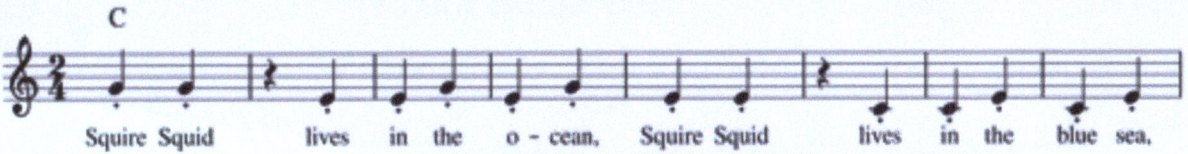
Squire Squid lives in the o-cean, Squire Squid lives in the blue sea,

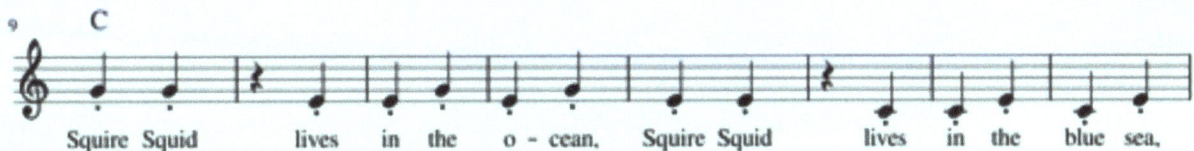
Squire Squid lives in the o-cean, Squire Squid lives in the blue sea,

La la la la la la la la la

La la la la la la la!

Meet the ...

Shy Shark

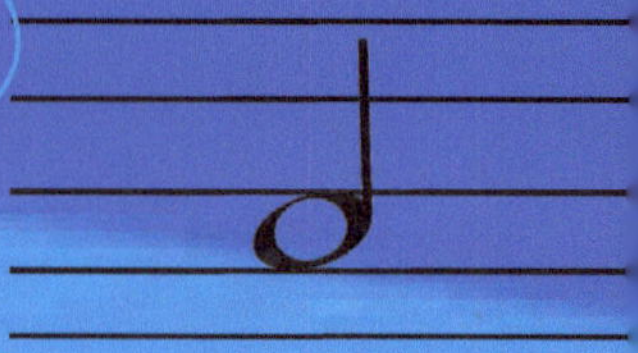

Swimming Shark

Under the Sea

Arranged by: F. Turnbull

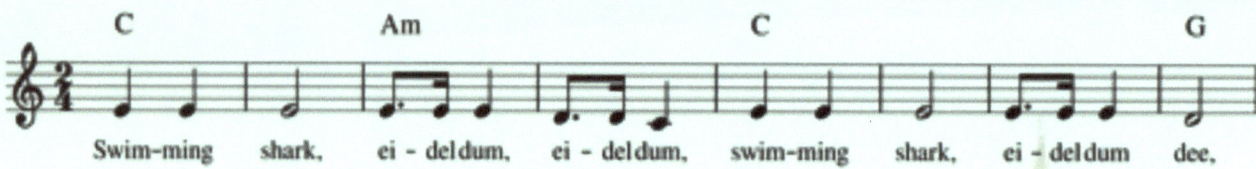

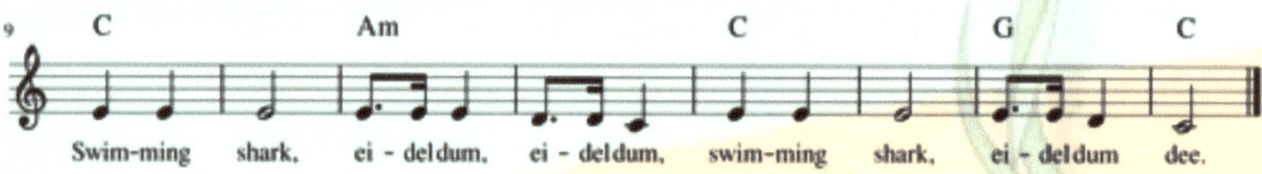

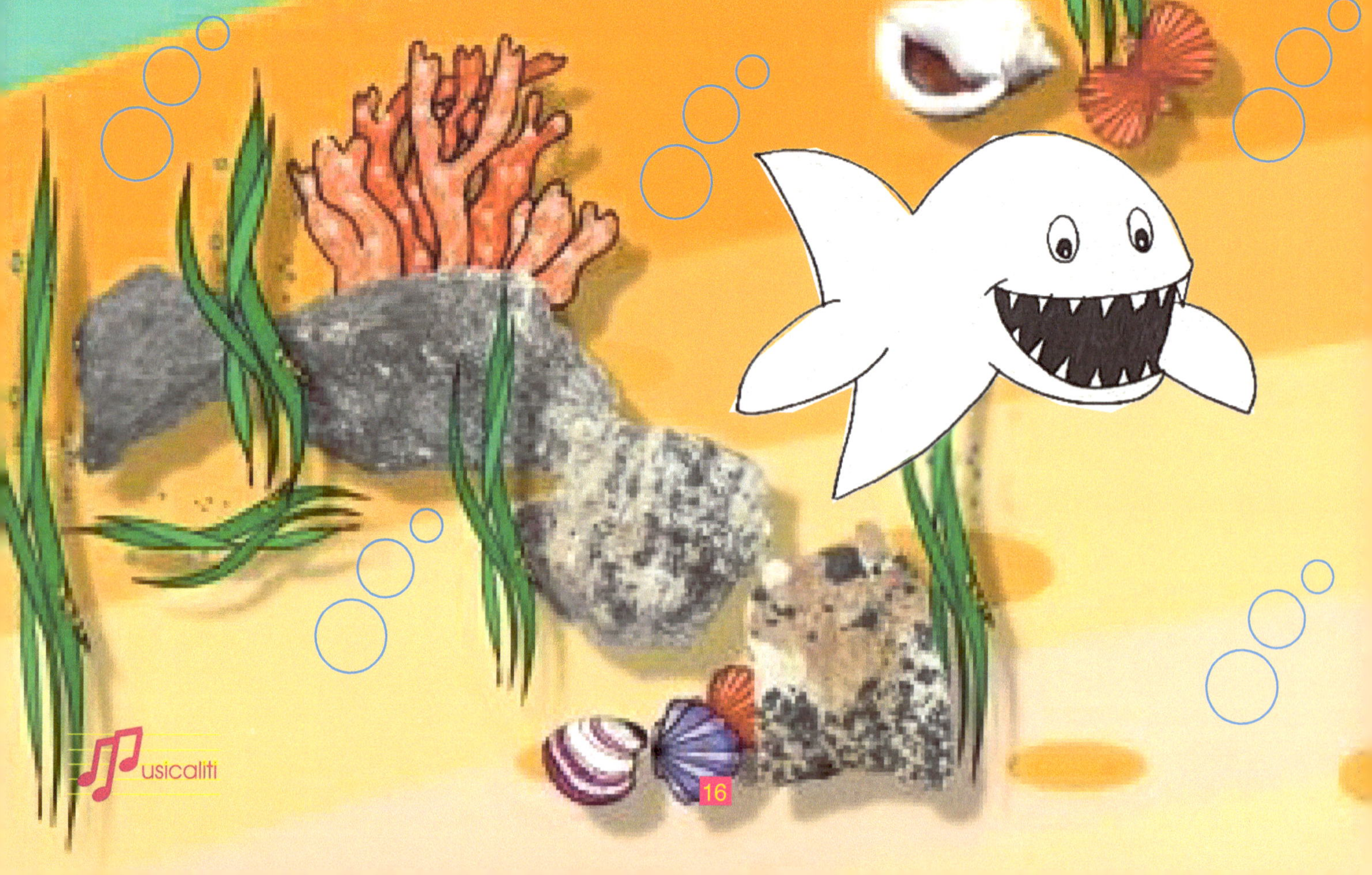

Sad Crab noticed another creature nearby, a beautiful shark! Being very shy, Shy Shark also hid away in the seaweed like Squire Squid.

When no-one else was around, he loved jumping out of the water.

One day, as he leaped through the surface of the water, he landed on a rock and broke his front tooth!

Sad Crab rushed over to help, calling Squire Squid over to pull Shy Shark back into the sea.

She told Shy Shark that she would need the best sea-surface jumper on her Great Adventure.

Immediately the three became best friends. Sad Crab was so happy that she changed her name to Glad Crab, and was really looking forward to going on their Great Adventure!

Under the Sea Song Book

Meet the ...
Green Fish

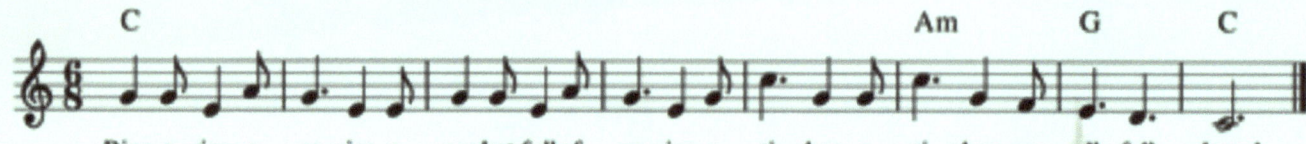

Ring a Rosies
Under the Sea

Arranged by F. Turnbull　　　　　　　　　　　　　　　　　　　　Traditional

Ring a ring a ro-sies, a pocket full of po-sies, a-ti-shoo, a-ti-shoo, we all fall down!

The three friends started out on their Great Adventure. While they were swimming, they saw a blurry green shape shoot past them like a flash of light!

Glad Crab held on to a nervous Squire Squid and Shy Shark tightly as they tried to swim away.

Hearing no sound at all, they suddenly saw a beautiful green fish swimming up and down, and then round and round, up and down, without a sound.

Glad Crab knew that she would need friends who could be quiet and quick, so she invited Green Fish to join the Crotchet Crew on their Great Adventure!

Frances Turnbull

Green Fish
Under the Sea

Composer: F. Turnbull

Green fish, green fish swim so quick, just like it's a par-ty trick,
up, down, round and round, but you ne-ver hear a sound!

Under the Sea Song Book

Meet the ...
Red Fish

Ickle Ockle
Under the Sea

Traditional   Arranged by: F. Turnbull

Ick - le ock - le, blue bot - tle, fi - shes in the sea,

if you want a part - ner, just choose me.

Green Fish, it turned out, was actually a mummy fish!

She had four identical baby fish, called quadruplets, and they were all red, and all swam together, wherever they went.

Playing Tig with each other, Glad Crab saw that got on well with each other. Even better, they could swim faster than anyone else.

She thought that they may be able to help everyone else, so invited them to join the group on their Great Adventure!

Frances Turnbull

Red Fish
Under the Sea

Composer: F. Turnbull

Lit-tle red fish swim, lit-tle red fish play, lit-tle fish play peep-bo, then they swim a-way,

Swim-ming, swim-ming, o-ver all the sea, swim-ming swim-ming, catch me if you please!

Under the Sea Song Book

Meet the ... Star Fish

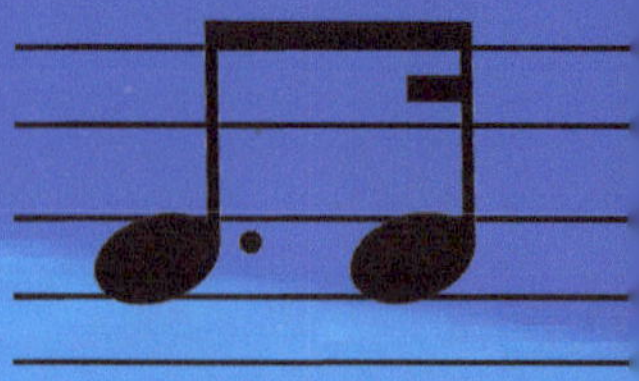

Row Your Boat
Under the Sea

Traditional Arranged by: F. Turnbull

Row, row, row your boat, gent-ly down the stream,
Rock, rock, rock your boat, gent-ly down the stream,
mer-ri-ly, mer-ri-ly, mer-ri-ly, mer-ri-ly, life is but a dream.
if you see a cro-co-di-le, don't for-get to scream!

Plop! Plop! Plop!

While the group of sea creatures were playing Tig, going on their Great Adventure, suddenly they saw little orange legs falling into the sea around them!

Oh, no! What could it be? Was it raining legs?

They were all amazed to see that slowly, the little legs grew bodies ... that grew four more legs!

Actually, it grew five arms, because it was a star fish!

The new Starfish Family joined the Crotchet Crew and Fish family on their Great Adventure!

Swimming ahead, Glad Crab looked at her huge posse and wondered who else she would need for a Great Adventure.

If anything tried to hurt them, only her sharp claws would be useful in an attack.

They needed someone who was brave. Someone who was strong. Someone who had been to ... the moon!

Suddenly they heard a big SPLASH! A rocket landed in the ocean, and out swam ... a TURTLE!

Brave with a super strong shell, he quickly agreed to join the Crotchet Crew on their Great Adventure!

Meet the ...

Octopus

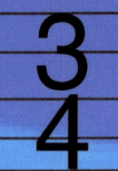

Clapping Land

Under the Sea

Traditional

Arranged by: F. Turnbull

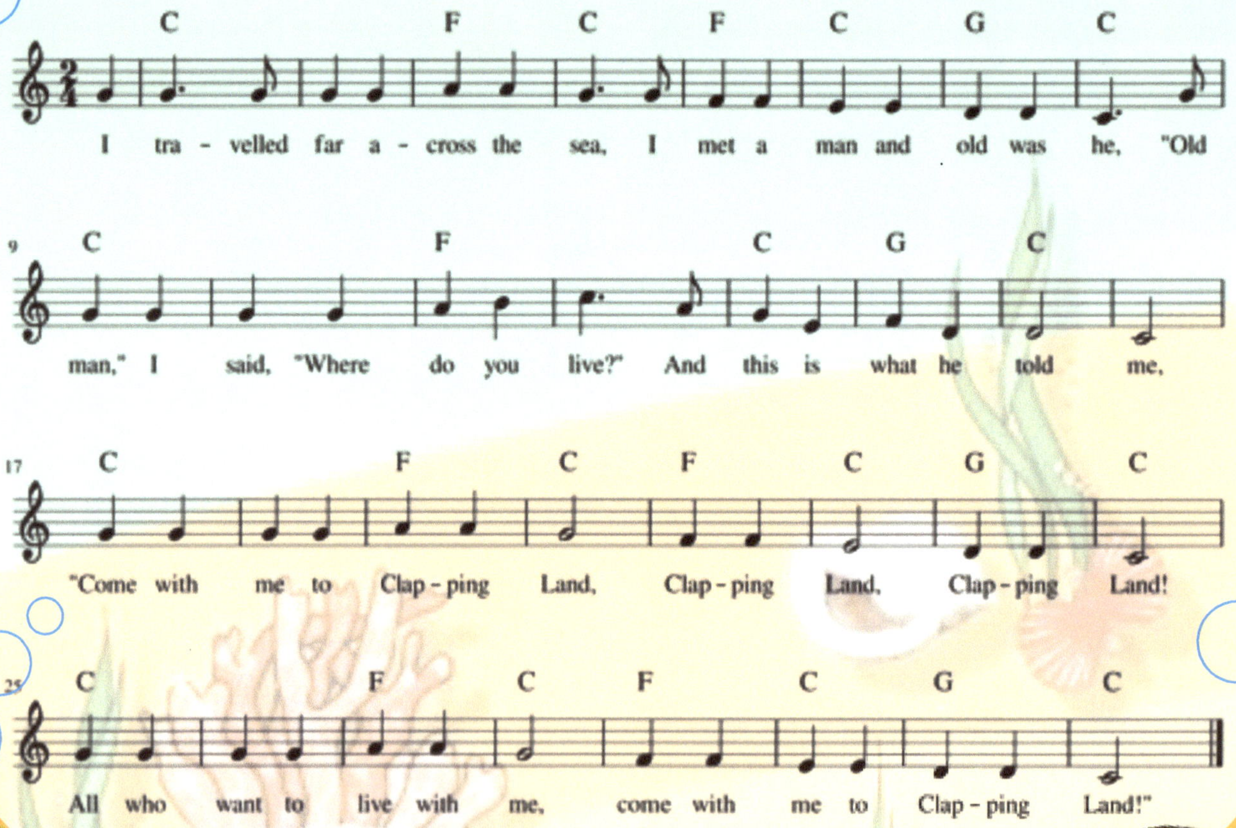
C F C F C G C
I tra - velled far a - cross the sea, I met a man and old was he, "Old
9
C F C G C
man," I said, "Where do you live?" And this is what he told me,
17
C F C F C G C
"Come with me to Clap - ping Land, Clap - ping Land, Clap - ping Land!
25
C F C F C G C
All who want to live with me, come with me to Clap - ping Land!"

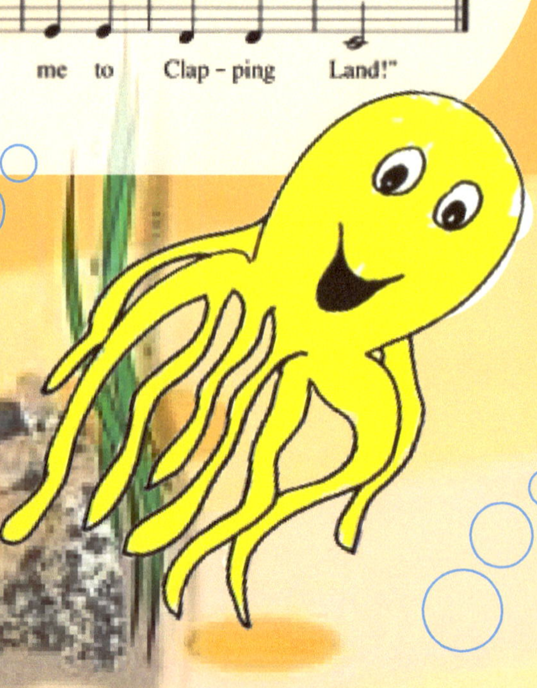

Glad Crab led the expedition - all of them were on a mission! Until they suddenly noticed that all the water around them had gone dark. Very, very dark. As the water cleared, Glad Crab, Squire Squid and Shy Shark quickly swam around the count all of their friends - but all they could see was turtle!

Who could have fish-napped eight friends? Squire Squid quietly, sneakily swam around a small coral reef to see ... Octopus! The eight-armed fiend had squirted ink around the friends and while nobody could see, grabbed the four little red fish, three star fish and one red fish in each tentacle!

Turtle quickly swam to the left; Shy Shark swam to the right; Glad Crab snapped her claws in anger! Around and around Octopus they all swam, around, and around, and around, until Octopus started feeling very, very dizzy.

Zip-zip-zip, all of the Red Fish quickly swam out of each tentacle, and without a sound, Green Fish joined them. The Starfish family broke the tentacle being held and swam back to their friends, leaving Glad Crab to speak to Octopus.

Octopus apologised for playing such a silly trick, saying she wanted to help on their Great Adventure!

Under the Sea Song Book

Meet the ...
Seahorse

My Paddle
Under the Sea

Traditional Arranged by: F. Turnbull

My pad - dle's keen and bright, fla - shing like sil - ver,

fol - low the wild goose flight, dip, dip, and swing!

All the friends were glad to be back together again, swimming, playing Tig, and seeking their fortune. Out of the corner of her eye, Octopus saw the most unique and magical underwater event: an underwater rainbow!

Now, we landlubbers with legs know that at the end of the rainbows are pots of gold, protected by Leprechauns, but undersea, the gold is protected by … Seahorses!

Everybody got into position, following the magical light of the underwater rainbow. Fish went to the left, while Starfish, Octopus and Turtle went to the right. Glad Crab led the group from the front, each of them wondering how scary Seahorse would be. Glad Crab swam closer, eyes looking everywhere at once for the scary, terrifying Seahorse … until … she felt … a … tap-tap-tap on her shoulder, and heard a little voice say, "TIG! YOU'RE IT!" A rainbow flash of light zoomed past as Seahorse swam away giggling. Glad Crab couldn't believe it – Seahorse just wanted to PLAY!

Quickly, the maddest game of Undersea Tig began, until all the sea creatures ended up in a tired, sleepy heap, laughing together.

"Here! Have some treasure!" said generous Seahorse, and Glad Crab was so pleased! A great end to a Great Adventure! "Come on friends, let's go home!" she said!

Seahorse

Under the Sea

Composer: F. Turnbull

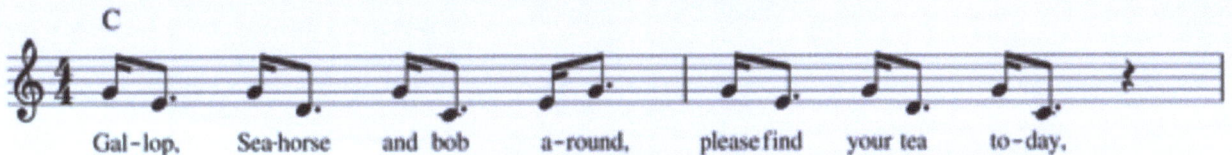

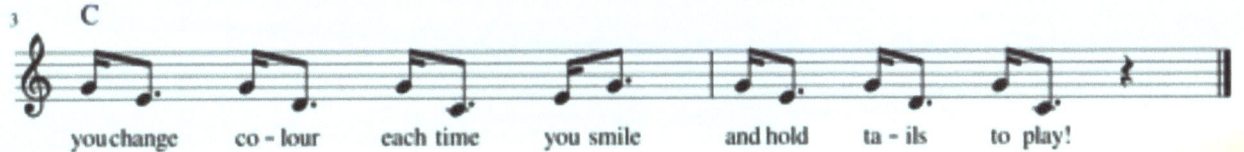

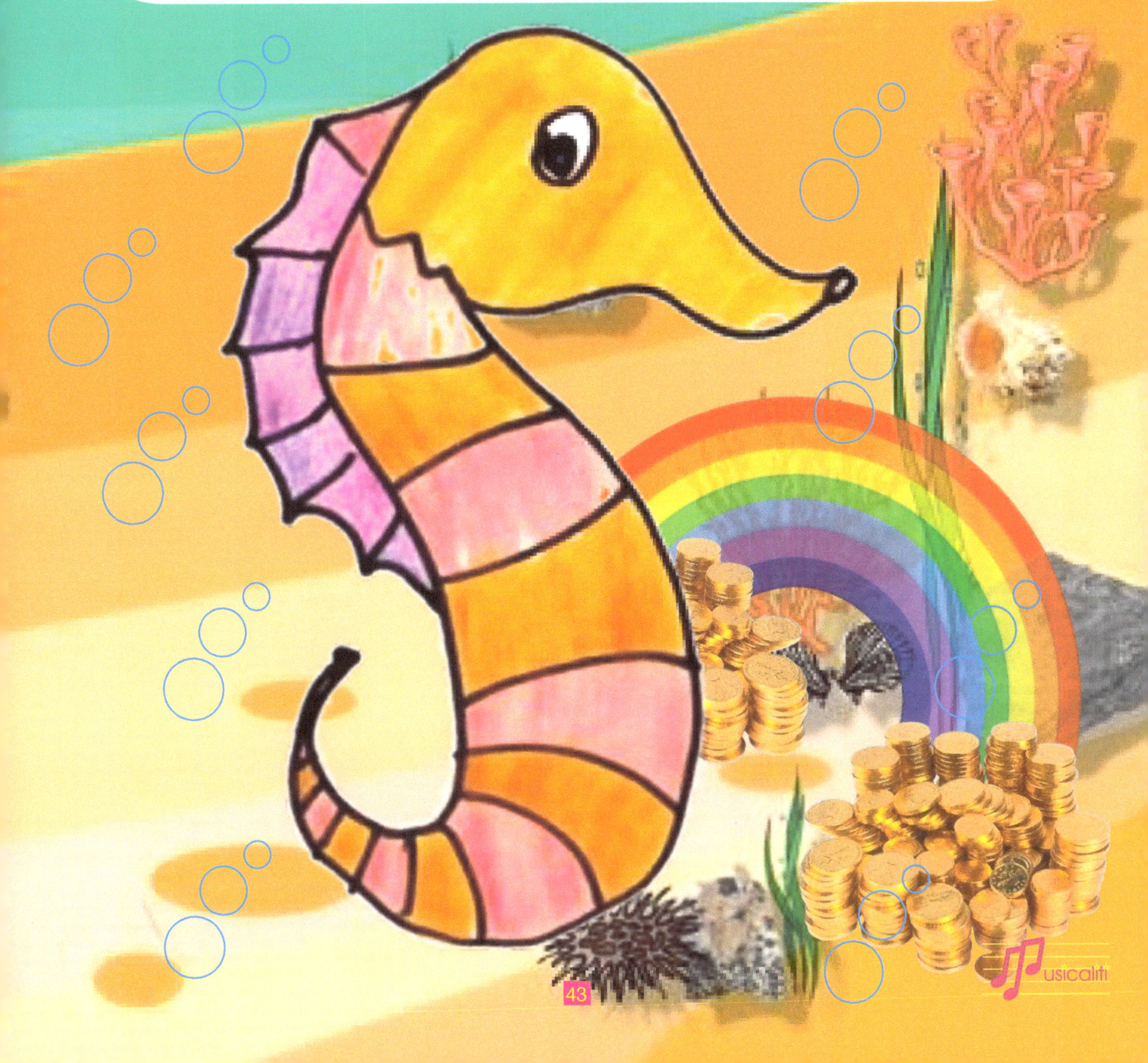

The happy party swam off quickly, an excited group of very different sea creatures who were very good at different things and had such a good time together!

Even Seahorse joined in on the journey, playing madly with the red fish until a dark cloud appeared overhead.

"It wasn't me!" Octopus said quickly, because everyone thought he had sprayed more ink, but no ... it was something bigger. Something far bigger than all of the friends together. It was ... a whale!

Everyone thought they were going to be eaten for sure, until the Seahorse, who spoke Whale language, said that she had said she knew of a secret undersea Kingdom.

Woo hoo! The undersea friends turned on their tails and went down to the magical Kingdom of Whales, where they lived happily ever after! What a Great Adventure!

My Song

Now use the music or fish pictures from the previous pages to make up your own song!

The End

Have you seen our other books?

Music Gone Wild Song Book:
Animal Songs for Ukulele
ISBN 9781907935688

Musical Munchies Song Book:
Food Songs for Ukulele
TBC

Passport to Transport Song Book:
Transport Songs for Ukulele
TBC

Goodies for Guitar:
90 songs for beginners
ISBN 9781907935695

Goodies for Guitar: Lvl 1
18 songs for beginners
ISBN 9781907935701

Goodies for Guitar: Lvl 2
20 songs for beginners
ISBN 9781907935718

Goodies for Guitar: Lvl 3
20 songs for beginners
ISBN 9781907935725

Goodies for Guitar: Lvl 4
10 songs for beginners
ISBN 9781907935732

Goodies for Guitar: Lvl 5
20 songs for beginners
ISBN 9781907935749

FIND US ON:

www.ingramcontent.com/pod-product-compliance
Lightning Source LLC
LaVergne TN
LVHW072113070426
835510LV00002B/31